STAGE
6
BOOK 1

NIGHT OF THE GHOST

John Townsend

RISING★STARS

To: Taz
Cc:
Subject: Good plan
From: Jack

New Message

Hi Taz,
I've got a plan. In the morning I'm going to stay in bed and take the day off school. When Gran goes out, I'll watch that scary DVD you gave me for Christmas.
How good is that?
Jack

Jack got a bag of flour and rubbed some into his face.
"I feel ill," he said feebly. "I've got bad stomach ache and I feel sick."

Gran didn't look up from the TV. "I know why," she said. "You ate too much spaghetti. You must be very tired from all your computer games, too. Go to bed and you'll feel fine in the morning."

Jack's plan wasn't going well.
"At school they told us to stay at home
if we don't feel well," he mumbled.

He pulled a sad face, but Gran still didn't look up. She was busy texting on her phone as she spoke, "I've got a bottle of medicine from the chemist. You'll soon feel better."

The next thing Jack knew, Gran was giving him a big spoonful.

"Ugh! That's ghastly stuff," he whined.

"You look a bit pale," she smiled. "As white as a ghoul!"

"What's a ghoul?" Jack asked.

"An evil sort of ghost. Like the one we get in this flat. I've never told you before but when I'm here on my own, I often see it."

"You can't frighten me. I'm as tough as a rhino," Jack grunted.

"I'll look at a bit of that DVD on my laptop now."

Jack slid under the bed covers and began to watch *Dead of Night*.

It was scary from the start. Drums beat louder and louder, like the rhythm of a heart. The main character was a zombie.

Suddenly the lights went off. There was a loud whoosh from outside his window. It seemed to echo around his room.

Then an evil whisper filled the darkness.
The window shook from a whack on the glass.

Jack froze with fear when a wheezy croak
came from outside.

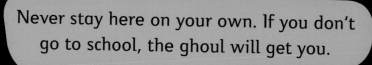

Never stay here on your own. If you don't
go to school, the ghoul will get you.

Jack crept to the window. He slowly put his hand on the curtain and pulled it back with a gasp.

A scary face stared in at him. He whimpered as a ghost whizzed away into the night.

Jack dived back under the bed covers in a mad panic.

Photo Browser S

Chat Attach Address Fonts Colors Save As Draft

To: Taz

Cc:

Subject: Good plan

From: Jack

+ New Message

New Message

To: Taz

Message:
Hi Taz.
I've got a new plan. I'll see you at the bus stop in the morning.
I'm going to school after all. I'll tell you why later.
Jack

Send   Cancel

19

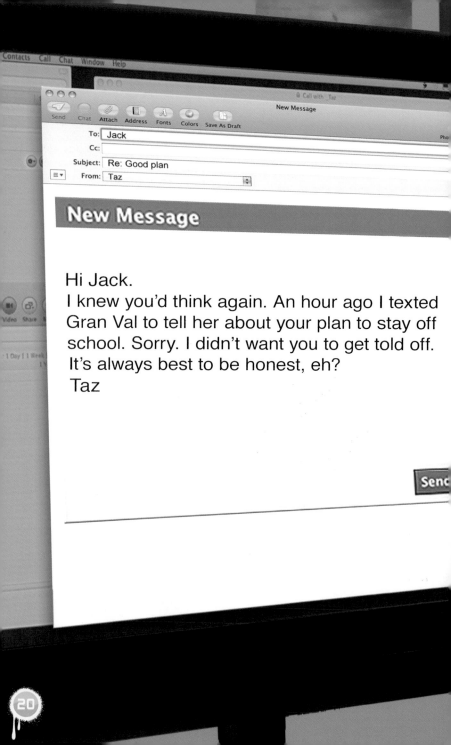

New Message

To: Jack
Cc:
Subject: Re: Good plan
From: Taz

New Message

Hi Jack.
I knew you'd think again. An hour ago I texted Gran Val to tell her about your plan to stay off school. Sorry. I didn't want you to get told off. It's always best to be honest, eh?
Taz

Show Stationery

Cancel

21

Sleep well, honest Jack!